EARTH
SCIENCE
PROJECTS
★ for kids ★

A PROJECT GUIDE TO

ROCKS
AND
MINERALS

Claire O'Neal

Mitchell Lane

P.O. Box 196
Hockessin, Delaware 19707
Visit us on the web: www.mitchelllane.com
Comments? email us: mitchelllane@mitchelllane.com

EARTH
SCIENCE
PROJECTS
★ for kids ★

A Project Guide to:
Earthquakes • Earth's Waters • **Rocks and Minerals** •
The Solar System • Volcanoes •
Wind, Weather and the Atmosphere

Copyright © 2011 by Mitchell Lane Publishers

Printing   2   3   4   5   6   7   8   9

PUBLISHER'S NOTE: The facts on which the story
in this book is based have been thoroughly
researched. Documentation of such research
can be found on page 44. While every possible
effort has been made to ensure accuracy, the
publisher will not assume liability for damages
caused by inaccuracies in the data, and
makes no warranty on the accuracy of the
information contained herein.

AUTHOR'S NOTE: The author gratefully
acknowledges the assistance of Dr. Michael
O'Neal, Kelly Van Camp, and the Iron Hill
Museum of Newark, Delaware.

Library of Congress
Cataloging-in-Publication Data

O'Neal, Claire.
  A project guide to rocks and minerals / by
Claire O'Neal.
    p. cm. — (Earth science projects for kids)
  Includes bibliographical references and
index.
  ISBN 978-1-58415-866-0 (lib. bd.)
  1. Rocks—Experiments—Juvenile literature. 2.
Minerals—Experiments—Juvenile literature. 3.
Geology—Juvenile literature. I. Title.
  QE432.2.O54 2010
  552.0078—dc22
                                        2010011158

eBook ISBN: 9781612281131

PLB / PLB2

CONTENTS

Introduction..4
Re-creating the Rock Cycle.....................................7
A Story Told in Sedimentary Rock.........................10
A Deposition Message in a Bottle.........................13
Instant Weathering 15
The Rocky Sponge..17
Become a Rock Hound 20
Mineral Detective Test 1: Looking for Clues..........23
Mineral Detective Test 2: Hardness and Streak....25
Mineral Detective Test 3: Specific Gravity 29
Mineral Detective Test 4: Become a
     Calcite Sleuth 31
Minerals From the Inside: Molecular Crystals.......33
Minerals From the Inside: Crystal Systems 35
Grow Your Own Crystals...38
Grow Your Own Salt Crystal Garden 40
Make Your Own Geode..42
Further Reading 44
     Books...44
     Works Consulted 44
     On the Internet 45
Science Supply Companies.....................................45
Glossary...46
Index...47

INTRODUCTION

Everywhere you look, you can see that rocks and minerals shape our world. From the lay of the land to the pebbles in a driveway, from mountains to valleys, from oceans to deserts—every landscape we know was formed from rocks and minerals.

We also depend on products made from rocks and minerals in our everyday lives. Limestone, granite, basalt, and marble form the buildings we use to work, study, shop, and play. Roads are filled with stone pieces, crushed and cemented back together to form a flat, durable surface. Cars, buses, trains, and airplanes are made using steel parts, copper wires, and lithium or lead batteries—all of which come from rocks mined from the earth.

A mineral is a solid, naturally occurring chemical compound that forms crystals. Gemstones are sparkling, valuable examples of how beautiful these crystals can be. Minerals also play important roles in biology. They help our bodies do an enormous variety of jobs, from maintaining strong bones (calcium) to copying our DNA (zinc) to delivering oxygen to all our cells (iron). Humans must ingest no less than 17 minerals on a daily basis to stay healthy.

Minerals combine to make rocks. Geologists classify rocks into three different categories, depending on how they were formed.

Igneous rocks formed from the cooling of magma. (*Igneous* means "fire".) They can be either plutonic or volcanic. Plutonic rocks (named after Pluto, the Roman god of the underworld) form under the surface of the earth when magma becomes trapped and cools slowly. Igneous

rocks with large crystals, such as granite, gabbro, and diolite, are made this way. Volcanic rocks (named after Vulcan, the Roman god of fire) form at Earth's surface when magma is pushed through a volcano. The magma, called lava when it reaches the surface, cools very quickly when exposed to air. Rocks with small crystals, such as basalt, andesite, and rhyolite, form this way. Some lava cools so quickly that crystals do not have time to form, producing "volcanic glass" such as obsidian, pumice, and scoria.

Sedimentary rocks are formed from sediments—dirt, dust, sand, shells, plants, animals, or anything that can be carried by water or wind. If sediment piles in one place and manages to stay there, eventually the top layers weigh so much that they press the layers below into rock, a process called lithification. Some sedimentary rocks form by cementation, which happens when chemicals make grains stick together. Many buildings are constructed from limestone or sandstone, or from concrete, which is made from ground-up sedimentary rocks.

Metamorphic rocks used to be sedimentary or igneous rocks, but were changed over long periods of time by forces of extreme heat and pressure. The end result makes a harder and stronger rock. Metamorphic rocks such as gneiss and schist look striped because layers of minerals in the parent rocks (such as granite) crystallized again or flattened. Slate—metamorphosed shale—is used to make durable roofs and walkways. Marble—metamorphosed limestone—is prized for its beauty in building stones and sculptures.

This book contains fascinating experiments you can do at home to learn more about rocks and minerals. Though simple to set up, each experiment encourages you to think like a scientist, asking questions and providing ideas to take your understanding to the next level. Whether for a school project or just for fun, you'll learn more about geology and science in general.

Many of the experiments need only common materials found around your home. Several experiments use household cleaners and hot liquids; please ask for **an adult**'s help with these. To explore the beautiful, orderly world of minerals later in this book, a kit with samples of basic rock-forming minerals is recommended. You might be able to borrow one from a nearby university, state geological survey, natural history museum, or high school that teaches earth science, or buy your own online for about $20. On page 45, find a list of trusted scientific supply companies from which to buy kits as well as less common materials.

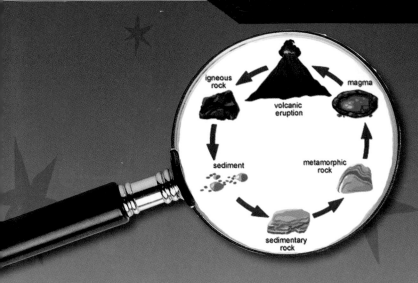

The diagram shows the rock cycle with labels: igneous rock, magma, volcanic eruption, metamorphic rock, sediment, sedimentary rock.

RE-CREATING THE ROCK CYCLE

Over time, Earth's powerful forces can change rocks from one group into new rock from another group. For example, igneous rock exposed to wind and water at the earth's surface will break down into sediment and perhaps become part of a new sedimentary rock. A metamorphic rock may become buried deep enough to melt, perhaps eventually hardening within pockets of magma into an igneous rock. Or a sedimentary rock could become buried at a site where Earth's heat and pressure can turn it into a metamorphic rock. This interchange is called the rock cycle.

While these types of changes happen over millions of years, you can study their effects in the span of a few minutes. Using crayons in place of rocks in the following experiment will allow you to model the rock cycle in your own kitchen.

Lava

7

MATERIALS

- crayons
- crayon sharpener
- small box or paper towel
- two pieces of heavy-duty aluminum foil, measuring 5" x 10" each
- **an adult**
- two small boards (2 x 4s or plywood)
- hammer
- oven
- aluminum pie pan
- timer
- pot holders

Make "minerals"—the constituents of all rocks—from crayon shavings. Sharpen several crayons, catching the shavings in a small box or on a paper towel. You will need enough shavings to make a pile about 3 inches long, 3 inches wide, and 1 inch deep. Sharpen crayons of a few different colors to represent the different minerals that make up rocks.

Double up the aluminum foil and place the "crayon sediment" on top. Form a packet to contain the sediment by folding the edges of the foil securely together.

Pretend these "mineral" pieces washed down a stream or settled on the bottom of an ocean. Lithify the sediment into sedimentary rock by pressing the packet flat with your hands on a flat surface. Gently open the foil and look at your "crayonite" rock.

Write down what you see. Is it still crumbly or flaky? Are there "grains" that haven't cemented yet?

Close the packet and take it outside. With **an adult**'s help, place the packet between two boards and hammer the top board several times. What does the rock look like now? How has your rock changed with the extra pressure? Just like the earth's lithification, the pressure exerted by your hands and the hammer cements the "mineral" grains together by squeezing out air and moisture.

Now let's turn your sedimentary rock into an igneous rock. Preheat an oven to 200°F. Place your closed foil packet in an aluminum pie pan. With **an adult**'s help, place the pie pan in the oven for 10 minutes. Using pot holders, take the pan out and let it cool for 15 minutes, then unwrap the foil packet. Your rock is now an igneous rock, changed by heat much as real rocks that have been exposed to magma. What did heat do to the rock? Rewrap the packet and return it to the oven for another 10 minutes. How has the heat changed the rock over time?

Create metamorphic conditions by exposing the igneous crayonite to both heat and pressure. Rewrap the foil packet and return it to the hot oven for 10 minutes. While it is still hot, use pot holders to press on the packet from the top or in from both sides. Let the packet cool before unwrapping your rock. Does your rock look different now? If so, how?

Three examples of "crayonite"—a rock made from crayon shavings using heat and pressure. Earth's forces create rock from sediment in a similar way.

A STORY TOLD IN SEDIMENTARY ROCK

Although sedimentary rock accounts for less than 7 percent of Earth's crust, it is the most common type of rock found on the surface. Sedimentary rocks were deposited in strata, or layers, throughout Earth's history by the same processes that are at work today. Strata follow a law called the principle of superposition, which simply means that older layers must have been deposited first, so they lie below younger layers. Strata therefore contain clues to what the earth was like long ago.

By looking at what minerals are within the rock layers, the types of grains present (silt, sand, clay), and whether or not the layers contain fossils, geologists can understand more about ancient Earth environments. As an environment changes, so do the minerals that are deposited there.

Here's an example scenario. Think of a spot, perhaps under the ocean. Bits of crushed seashells, sand, silt, and clay sink to the ocean bottom, eventually forming limestone. Perhaps over time, Earth gets warmer, sea level rises, and that same spot is now deeper underwater. The location is quieter now; more silt, fewer seashells, and less sand sink to the bottom, and siltstone forms instead. Perhaps over time,

Earth cools, and the ocean gets much shallower at the spot. Greater action from currents creates coarser deposits of sand, pebbles, and even fossils from animals that died along the shore, forming sandstone. Perhaps over more time, Earth cools further, trapping water in ice and glaciers on the land and causing the ocean to get much shallower at that spot. Plants and animals thrived and died in the gooey mud, where their remains will eventually turn to coal. Perhaps over time, freshwater returned to the spot, flushing out the swamp and creating a new river environment for sandstone deposition.

You can re-create this scenario in your own rock strata made out of gelatin, watching the principle of superposition for yourself.

MATERIALS

- clear Pyrex or glass 13" x 9" baking dish
- cooking spray
- measuring cup (2-cup size)
- mixing bowl
- 1 box (4 envelopes) unflavored gelatin (like Knox, or use lime gelatin)
- 1 3-ounce package each of red and orange gelatin (like Jell-O)
- teakettle and stove
- **an adult**
- timer
- 2 3-ounce packages of yellow gelatin
- 1 8-ounce tub whipped topping (like Cool Whip)
- water
- whisk
- refrigerator
- 1 banana, chopped into small pieces
- 6 whole graham crackers, crushed into crumbs
- green or brown frosting
- mini marshmallows
- candy creatures
- spoon

Coat the bottom and sides of a baking dish with cooking spray.

Make a layer of "limestone" using the following recipe for opaque white gelatin to mimic limestone's natural color (or, alternatively, use lime gelatin). In the mixing bowl, add two envelopes of unflavored gelatin to ¾ cup cold water. Let the powder sit for 1 minute. With **an adult**'s help, add ¾ cup boiling water, stirring until the gelatin dissolves. Cool for 15 minutes, then whisk in half the tub of whipped topping. Pour the mixture into the baking dish and refrigerate until firm (about 2 hours).

Make a layer of red "siltstone" to spread on top of the limestone. Combine the contents of the red gelatin package with ¾ cup boiling water and stir to dissolve the powder. Add ¾ cup cold water and cool for 15 minutes. Whisk in 1 cup whipped topping. Pour the mixture into the baking dish to form an even layer atop the limestone. Return the dish to the refrigerator until the top layer is firm (about 2 hours).

Make a layer of orange "sandstone" by adding the contents of the orange gelatin package to ¾ cup boiling water and stirring to dissolve the powder. Add ¾ cup cold water, then cool the mixture in the refrigerator until the gelatin just begins to firm (1 to 2 hours). At this point, gently stir in edible fossils. Use mini marshmallows as shells, banana pieces as bone fragments, or soft-candy creatures as animals that died long ago and became fossils. Gently pour the fossil-rich "sandstone" mixture into the baking dish, smoothing out the layer with a spoon. Return the dish to the refrigerator until the sandstone is firm (about 1 hour).

Top the sandstone with a thick "coal" layer of graham cracker crumbs. Prepare 1 envelope of unflavored gelatin with ⅓ cup cold water and ⅓ cup boiling water. Let it sit for 15 minutes before pouring it over the crumbs. Return the dish to the refrigerator to cement the coal together (about 1 hour).

End with a layer of yellow "sandstone." Combine the yellow (lemon) gelatin package contents with ¾ cup boiling water and stir to dissolve the powder. Add ¾ cup cold water and let it cool for about 15 minutes. Transfer the mixing bowl to the fridge until the gelatin is almost firm. Mix in graham cracker crumbs to make the layer really sandy. Transfer the mixture to the baking dish, and chill the finished gelatin layers in the refrigerator for another 2 hours. Top off your layers with some frosting to represent grass (green) or surface dirt (chocolate).

Cut a big slice for you and your friends and admire the layers. This experiment takes a few hours (over perhaps two days), but that's nothing compared to the few hundred million years it would take to create the same scenario in rocks.

A DEPOSITION MESSAGE IN A BOTTLE

Sedimentary rock is made of sediment, or grains. Each originally came from another rock that was broken down over time by wind or water in a process called erosion. Wind or water brought the grains together, and then deposited them in the same place at the same time. Over time, the grains lithified to become rock.

Sedimentary rocks are classified by the size of their grains. Conglomerate and breccia have the largest grains, where a "large" grain can mean anywhere from pebble- to boulder-sized. In contrast, shale has the smallest grains, made of clay particles so small that you can't see them without a microscope.

The environmental conditions of a particular spot determine what kind of grains might be deposited there. High-energy conditions— landslides, fast-moving riverbeds, glaciers, ocean tides—can move large grains. Low-energy conditions—deep water, slow winds—cannot. To form a deposit, the energy in an environment has to be low enough to allow sediment to settle, or stay put.

Grain size alone—not the makeup of the grains—determines settling rates. Geologists divide grain size into the following categories: gravel, sand, silt, and clay.

You can investigate settling rates by creating your own depositional environment. What class of sedimentary rock will you form?

MATERIALS

¤ two handfuls each of aquarium gravel, play sand, soil
¤ pan or baking dish
¤ empty plastic 2-liter bottle
¤ funnel
¤ water
¤ timer
¤ stirring stick

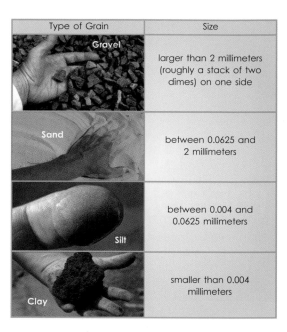

Type of Grain	Size
Gravel	larger than 2 millimeters (roughly a stack of two dimes) on one side
Sand	between 0.0625 and 2 millimeters
Silt	between 0.004 and 0.0625 millimeters
Clay	smaller than 0.004 millimeters

Break up the dirt over a pan or baking dish. Remove any rocks, animals, or plants. Let it air out until the dirt is dry to the touch.

Place a funnel atop an empty 2-liter plastic bottle. Carefully add the gravel, sand, and dirt to the bottle. Fill the bottle almost all the way with water.

Cap the bottle and shake well. After all particles are suspended in the water, continue shaking for about a minute more.

Place the bottle on a flat surface and start the timer. Watch the bottle carefully. Which sediment size falls to the bottom first? How long does it take? Watch the bottle regularly over the course of three days and note what you see.

Repeat the experiment, but this time pretend that a high-energy force enters the deposition environment (such as a strong current from a hurricane or flood). After one sediment layer forms, carefully stir only the liquid so as not to disturb the already settled grains. How much longer does it take to see the same layers?

INSTANT WEATHERING

It's hard to imagine that one little raindrop could have any effect on something as big, durable, and hard as a rock. But to a rock exposed to millions of rainstorms over time, a raindrop looks more like a chainsaw! When raindrops hit, water flows, or ice freezes, constant and small impacts wear rocks away bit by bit.

This process is called mechanical weathering. In mechanical weathering, brute force, no matter how small, tears rocks apart. Rocks can also be broken apart by chemical reactions in a process called chemical weathering. Cave formation is a familiar example of chemical weathering, where acidic compounds in groundwater dissolve bedrock limestone, eating holes through the solid rock.

In nature, weathering happens slowly. You can speed up the process and observe it yourself in a matter of hours.

MATERIALS

- 15 small sedimentary rocks— limestone, sandstone, or shale
- 5 paper towels
- 5 empty wide-mouth plastic bottles with lids (such as Gatorade or Nalgene)
- 5 clear jars
- permanent marker
- water
- vinegar
- tongs
- camera (optional)

Separate the rocks into five groups by placing three rocks on separate paper towels. Label the paper towels A through E. Label the bottles and jars similarly.

Half fill plastic bottles A through D with water. Half fill the E bottle with vinegar.

Place the rocks on the A paper towel in the A bottle; B paper towel rocks in the B bottle, and so on. Cap all the bottles except E. Set the A bottle aside—it will be the control.

Mimic mechanical weathering from water. Shake the B bottle vigorously up and down for three minutes (rest when you need to!). Remove the rocks from the bottle with tongs and place them back on the B towel. Note and/or take pictures of what they look like now. Swirl the liquid in the B bottle around to suspend loose particles, then empty the bottle into the B jar.

Repeat the process for the C jar, except this time shake the bottle for 30 seconds.

Mimic mechanical weathering from ice. Place the D bottle in your freezer and leave it there until ice forms around the rock. Take the bottle out and let it thaw at room temperature. Return the bottle to the freezer and repeat until loose sediment is visible in the water. How many freeze-thaw cycles did it take?

Look at the E bottle. Sedimentary rocks contain calcite, which dissolves in acid. When calcite-containing rocks—especially limestone—are exposed to acid, bubbles will form on the rock surface. What is happening to your rocks? How long does the reaction continue?

To investigate further, repeat the weathering experiments using igneous and metamorphic rocks. Do you think your results will be different? Why or why not?

THE ROCKY SPONGE

"Solid as a rock," the old saying goes. But actually, all rocks have holes or cracks, ranging from enormous to microscopic. These holes contribute to a rock's porosity, or the percentage of the rock's volume that is open space. That space can hold fluid, such as air, water, or oil.

How a rock forms determines its porosity. For example, pumice, the most porous rock, forms from exploding lava, which has a lot of air bubbles. The result looks more like foam than rock. With porosity values of up to 85 percent—meaning only 15 percent is rock—pumice can even float!

However, most igneous and metamorphic rocks are not very porous. When they form, empty spaces are filled in or squeezed out. In contrast, sedimentary rocks are quite porous. The gentler, slower nature of lithification allows the rock to form with spaces between grains.

Porosity is very important to industries that use rock. Road construction projects need gravels made out of low-porosity rock to keep the finished road from cracking during an icy winter. Kitchen designers choose low-porosity granite countertops because more porous rocks could trap food-contaminating bacteria. However, porous rocks certainly have importance. Water collects in porous rock, making underground reservoirs that hold most of our drinking water. And the largest oil field in the world—Ghawar in Saudi Arabia—lies above a limestone deposit estimated to have above 30 percent porosity in some places.

You can see for yourself how a rock can act like a sponge with the following porosity test. Remember to take careful notes about the weight and look of the rocks and the volumes of water you use.

MATERIALS

- 2 identical clear plastic containers, large enough to hold each of the following materials one at a time: brick, limestone, sandstone, pumice, natural sponge or loofa
- metric scale (preferably digital)
- water
- 500 ml beaker or graduated cylinder
- pencil
- notebook
- marker
- ruler

Weigh the brick and record its mass in your notebook, as well as other observations: What color is it? How does it feel in your hand?

Place the brick in one of the plastic containers. Using the beaker, measure and add enough water to completely cover the brick. Draw a line on the outside of the container to show the water's level. Measure its height using the ruler, and record your findings.

Soak the brick for 45 minutes.

Meanwhile, add an identical amount of water to the empty container. Mark the water's height and measure it.

Take out the brick and allow the surface water to run back into the container. Mark and measure the water level again. How does it compare to the level in the second container?

Weigh the brick. If it absorbed water, it will weigh more than it did before.

Measure the amount of water remaining in the first container to find out how much water the brick absorbed.

Repeat all these steps using the other types of stones and the natural sponge. How do they compare and why? Because these materials will have different masses to begin with, make sure you compare their changes in mass. You can express this value as a percentage:

mass after soaking ÷ mass before soaking × 100 = % change in mass

Rocks like this porous pumice sample absorb a surprising amount of water.

BECOME A
ROCK HOUND

Rocks and minerals are fun to collect. Any rock collection captures pieces of the earth's history that are thousands or millions of years old. Even rocks from ordinary places can be beautiful, unusual, valuable, and long-lasting.

Rock collectors call themselves rock hounds. Like hound dogs drawn to a scent, rock hounds are drawn to rocks. Many adult earth scientists were rock hounds as kids. Rock collecting requires a scientist's mind—taking samples, keeping records, and trying to understand more about the earth around you. However, because collecting rocks is easy, fun, and free, people from all backgrounds and careers can enjoy rock collecting as a hobby.

MATERIALS

- a bag or backpack
- notebook and pen or pencil
- hand lens (magnifying glass)
- zip-top bags
- plastic tub
- dish soap
- old toothbrush
- correction fluid (such as White-Out)
- egg cartons (empty)
- newspaper
- sturdy box (such as a shoebox)
- permanent marker
- camera (optional)
- field guide to rocks and minerals

Pack a bag or backpack with a notebook and pen, hand lens, and some zip-top bags. Take it to a driveway, a nearby stream, or anywhere else small rocks are lying on the ground. Be sure to get permission to collect rocks if you plan to enter someone else's property. Pick out some pebbles whose shapes, colors, or feel interests you. Take notes. What does each rock look like? Note its color, stripes, or spots. How big is it? Why did you choose it? Inspect the rocks with the hand lens and write down what you see. Place each rock inside a zip-top bag labeled with the date and location.

At home, give your rocks a bath. Fill a plastic tub with cold, soapy water. One at a time, remove each rock from its bag and wash it. If your rock is not too delicate, scrub it with an old toothbrush to get all the grime off. Lay each rock out to dry. Note how the rocks look now—once clean and dry, they may look very different than when you found them. Record your observations in your notebook.

Dab a spot of correction fluid on each rock. Let the spot dry, then write a label on it with a permanent marker. Copy the label into your notebook, next to your notes about that rock. Place each rock in its own well of an egg carton. If the rock is big, wrap it in newspaper and keep it in a shoebox.

Organize your collection. There are as many ways to do this as there are rock collectors! You can organize your rocks by color, size, date, or place found. As you gain experience identifying your specimens, you can also group your collections by rock type or mineral type.

Now open your collector's eyes to the world around you.

Find interesting rocks on trails when you go hiking or walking in the woods. When you're in the car, ask your parents if they will pull over when you see piles of rocks beside the road.

Take pictures of interesting rock formations or of sites where you've collected. As your understanding of geology grows, knowing more about a site may help you identify your specimens.

Visit natural history museums or your state geological survey to learn more about rocks, minerals, and fossils. Call or e-mail a staff member to see if he or she could help you learn more about your specimens or give you tips on collecting in your area. Seek out a local rock collector's club. Learn from other collectors and ask to join them on rock hunts. Attend a scientific meeting, like those held by the Geological Society of America. Many professionals love to share their interests with eager students.

A rock hound's tool kit is never complete without a field guide to rocks and minerals. Use your field guide to find out more about each type of rock and mineral you find.

The next experiments show you how to perform simple tests that geologists use to identify rocks and minerals. Compare your results with field guides and reference books to confidently identify the common rock-forming minerals.

Look for interesting rocks for your collection in streams at a local park, on roadsides, at the beach, or even your own backyard.

MINERAL DETECTIVE TEST 1: LOOKING FOR CLUES

Learning what your own samples are will help you piece together clues about where they came from, and what stories the geology of your area has to tell. But identifying rocks and minerals can be tricky, even for professionals. Of the more than 3,500 different kinds of minerals, many look alike or have similar properties. Don't despair! Most minerals are extremely rare. It's likely that only a few extremely common minerals make up the rocks in your area. Compare your rock collection to a standard kit of minerals to analyze a few important characteristics in your rocks.

MATERIALS
- ¤ rock samples, such as those in your collection
- ¤ standard set of minerals (such as one from American Educational Products, at http://www.amep.com/ standarddetail.asp?cid=160)
- ¤ hand lens
- ¤ notebook and pen or pencil

Explore your rock and mineral collection with a hand lens to appreciate the beauty of the crystal world. For example, only under magnification can you see the perfect cubes formed by individual crystals in this pyrite sample.

Write down each mineral's color. Color can be handy for identification, but remember that many minerals have similar colors, and some can rust or change color over time.

Determine the luster, a technical word for a mineral's shine. Metallic luster means a mineral looks opaque and shiny, like metal. Naturally, gold and silver have a metallic luster, but so do pyrite, magnetite, and hematite. Other minerals have a nonmetallic luster. Nonmetallic luster can be further divided into vitreous, silky, pearly, and even greasy lusters. Gemstones have a vitreous luster, which means they are transparent like glass.

Note the rock or mineral's crystal shape, drawing pictures of what the individual crystals of the rock look like. Minerals also have a crystal habit, which is how the individual crystals arrange themselves. For example, silver crystals form in delicate branches, while muscovite mica forms as stacks of thin plates.

Now look at each sample with the hand lens. Can you make out individual crystals or grains? What do they look like?

Take notes on anything else that catches your eye.

MINERAL DETECTIVE TEST 2: HARDNESS AND STREAK

German mineralogist Friedrich Mohs (1773–1839) used common sense to develop a test for hardness. He knew that a harder mineral will scratch a softer one. The Mohs scale ranges from 1 (softest) to 10 (hardest).

Talc, which easily crumbles to powder, scores 1, while diamond, one of the hardest substances on Earth, scores 10. Measure the hardness of your rocks and minerals.

MATERIALS

- an adult
- rocks and minerals
- penny
- stainless steel knife
- sandpaper
- corundum paper
- notebook and pen or pencil

Mohs Hardness Scale

Talc	Gypsum	Calcite	Fluorite	Apatite
1	**2**	**3**	**4**	**5**

very soft like chalk	easily scratched with a nail	difficult to scratch with a nail	cannot be scratched with a nail	about the hardness of teeth

Feldspar	Quartz	Topaz	Ruby	Diamond
6	**7**	**8**	**9**	**10**
suitable for gems	scratches glass	harder than quartz	harder than topaz	hardest material known to man

Under **adult** supervision, scratch each rock and mineral specimen with the following, in order: your fingernail, a penny, a knife blade, sandpaper, and corundum paper. What does your sample scratch? What scratches it? Write down your results.

Determine a range of possible hardness values for your samples. For example, if you can scratch a mineral with a penny but not a knife, it must have a hardness value between 3.5 and 5.5. Now try scratching it with fluorite. If that works, its hardness must be between 3.5 and 4.

Mineralogists also use streak to identify minerals. Streak is the color a rock or mineral leaves behind when it is dragged across an unglazed porcelain tile. Mineral streaks can be white, gray/black, yellow, green, red, or blue.

To perform the hardness test, scratch the rocks in your collection with objects of known hardness. This sample of talc (rating 1 on the Mohs hardness scale) is easily scratched with a copper penny.

You can test the streak of local rock and mineral samples.

MATERIALS

- ¤ 2 identical nails
- ¤ 2 pennies
- ¤ 2 glass jars
- ¤ vinegar
- ¤ unglazed porcelain tile (found at ceramics shops and art stores)
- ¤ rocks and minerals

Soak one nail and one penny in a jar of vinegar until they are rusted.

Drag the nails across the tile one at a time and record the results. What color are the streaks? Repeat for the pennies. Rusting occurs at the surface; it does not change the makeup, or composition, of the nail and penny. Streak reveals information specific to a mineral's composition.

Drag your rocks and minerals, one at a time, across the tile. Record your results. If you have any of the following minerals, compare their streaks with your unknown specimens:

hematite—dark red
quartz, calcite, gypsum—white to colorless
pyrite—brown
hornblende—green
graphite, galena, magnetite—gray to black

Test for streak by rubbing a rock sample against an unglazed ceramic tile. Streaks of some pure minerals, from left to right: hematite, pyrite, sulfur, and galena.

MINERAL DETECTIVE TEST 3: SPECIFIC GRAVITY

Pick up a rock. Is it heavy? Most rocks feel heavy for their size, but if you pick up a second rock, you might notice that it feels heavier or lighter than the first. Mineralogists refer to this property as heft. In a lab, the technical term for it is *specific gravity*. Specific gravity is a measure of density, which is the mass of an object divided by its volume. Density tells you how tightly molecules are packed inside a substance.

Specific gravity compares the density of a substance to the density of water, which has a specific gravity of 1.0. Objects with higher specific gravities are heavy for their size. Miners consider anything above 2.9 to be heavy. Famously heavy minerals include lead (7.5) and platinum (21.4). These numbers mean, for example, that a platinum nugget of a certain volume is 21.4 times heavier than the same volume of water. Lighter minerals have low specific gravities. Graphite, used in pencil lead, has a specific gravity of 2.1.

Let's take your rock and mineral samples for a dip in a graduated cylinder to reveal their specific gravities.

MATERIALS

- ¤ Unknown rock and mineral samples of similar sizes
- ¤ Two or three known mineral samples, such as gypsum (specific gravity = 2.3), calcite (2.7), magnetite (5.2)
- ¤ metric scale (preferably digital)
- ¤ water
- ¤ graduated cylinder large enough to accommodate rock samples
- ¤ towel
- ¤ calculator
- ¤ notebook
- ¤ pencil

Which of your rock samples do you think has the lowest specific gravity? The highest? You won't be able to predict exact specific gravity values, but you can use the heft test to make an educated guess. Pick up two samples at a time and compare how heavy they feel to each other. List the samples in order from least to greatest heft. Use the known samples to guide you. Try to ignore differences in sample size.

Make sure your samples are completely dry. Place each rock or mineral on a scale and record its mass.

Fill a graduated cylinder halfway with water. Record the water's volume. Place one rock or mineral sample in the graduated cylinder. Record the new water volume, then take it out and dry it off.

Calculate the sample's specific gravity as follows:

Subtract the second volume reading from the first. This number is the volume of the sample, in milliliters.

Divide the sample's mass by its volume. This number is the specific gravity.

Repeat the experiment for each sample.

Compare your results with known values for quartz, calcite, and magnetite. Are they close? If not, where do you think errors may have come from?

Compare your results to the heft test you did at the beginning of the experiment. How accurate was the heft test? How small of a difference in specific gravity can you detect by the heft test?

MINERAL DETECTIVE TEST 4:
BECOME A CALCITE SLEUTH

Calcite—calcium carbonate—is the most abundant mineral on earth. Living things use calcite in shells or bones, and it forms the cement that glues together many sedimentary rocks. Limestone forms on the ocean floor from ground-up seashells, so it is especially rich in calcite. You might also eat calcite when you have a stomachache—it's the active ingredient in many antacids.

The acid test makes calcite one of the easiest minerals to identify. Just a few drops of an acid on a sample of calcite will create instant fizz. Carbon dioxide bubbles up as the acid frees calcium from the rock. In the field, geologists use the acid test to tell limestone from dolomite. These rocks look the same, but add acid to limestone and it fizzes wildly, while dolomite fizzes weakly.

Hydrochloric acid is the weapon of choice for field geologists, but it is poisonous. The following experiment uses vinegar instead. Because it is a weaker acid, you may need to repeat the experiments using hot vinegar if you aren't successful the first time.

MATERIALS

- vinegar
- glass jar
- calcite
- eyedropper or medicine dropper
- limestone
- sandstone
- marble
- dolomite
- hand lens or magnifying glass
- unknown rock samples
- seashell
- clean chicken bones

Pour some vinegar into a glass jar. Add a small chunk of calcite. What happens?

Drop vinegar onto the surface of the limestone, marble, and dolomite. Look closely at the drop site with your hand lens. What happens? Which samples creates the most bubbles?

Drop vinegar onto the surface of some unknown rock samples. With larger specimens, test several spots. Do any react?

If you like, repeat these tests with different acids, such as lemon juice or different strengths of vinegar. You can also use hydrochloric acid—sold in dropper bottles with many rock kits—if you have rubber gloves and **an adult** to help out. Which acid creates the strongest reactions?

The acid in the vinegar reacts with calcium in living things, too. Remember that limestone forms from ground-up seashells. Add a seashell to a jar of vinegar. What happens?

Your bones (and a chicken's) contain calcium. Place a few chicken bones in a glass jar and cover them with vinegar. Place the lid on the jar and let it sit for three days. Take the bones out and bend them. Yes, bend them, like rubber! The vinegar dissolved the calcium in the bones, leaving behind only soft tissue. Your bones need calcium to keep their shape. Think of that the next time your mom tells you to drink your milk or eat your spinach.

Calcite

MINERALS FROM THE INSIDE: MOLECULAR CRYSTALS

Minerals are chemical compounds that form when one or more elements come together. Table salt, for example, comes from a mineral called halite, made when a chlorine atom pairs with a sodium atom. That couple attracts others like it, and the pairs arrange themselves in a repeating pattern to make a crystal. Because each mineral is made of different arrangements of elements, each produces a crystal unique to that mineral.

Crystals begin growing at the smallest possible level, when two molecules of a mineral happen to bump into each other in just the right way. You can see what a crystal looks like at the molecular level by building a ball-and-stick model of a halite crystal.

MATERIALS
- ¤ modeling clay in two colors (we'll call them A and B)
- ¤ toothpicks
- ¤ protractor

Shape the A clay into 14 equal-sized balls. These represent sodium atoms. Shape the B clay into 13 equal-sized balls. These represent chlorine atoms.

Create bonds using toothpicks. Attach one A ball and one B ball to opposite ends of each of 13 toothpicks, with one A ball left over. In an actual salt molecule, attraction between the chlorine and the sodium creates the bond, much as two opposite ends of a magnet attract each other.

Build a 3 atom x 3 atom x 3 atom cube. Connect the pairs with empty toothpicks, using your protractor to measure 90-degree angles. Ensure that an A always connects to a B. Your leftover A ball will finish the cube. The end result will look like the one in the photo below.

Let your structure harden overnight.

If you could look at a halite (salt) crystal on the smallest possible scale, this is what you would see—a pattern of alternating sodium (black) and chloride (white) atoms, held in place by chemical bonds (toothpicks).

MINERALS FROM THE INSIDE: CRYSTAL SYSTEMS

Look at a mineral crystal, such as a sparkling diamond. The chemistry between the mineral's atoms explains how nature could make a perfect cube. As a mineral's molecules group together, atoms between molecules require a fixed amount of space in order to interact. The angles and distances of these interactions determine the shape in which a crystal will form. All minerals belong to one of the seven crystal systems:

¤ Isometric crystals are the most symmetrical. All sides have the same dimensions; all angles between the sides are the same. Common isometric crystals include halite and pyrite, which form cubes. Garnet, a semiprecious gemstone mineral, forms 12-sided isometric crystals called dodecahedrons.

¤ Hexagonal crystals form triangles or hexagons. Quartz and calcite are common examples of hexagonal minerals. Water also crystallizes in a hexagonal system to form ice.

¤ Tetragonal crystals are like cubes elongated in one direction. Zircon—a mineral prized both as a gemstone and as an insulator in nuclear reactors—forms tetragonal crystals.

¤ Trigonal or rhombohedric crystals are cubes that have been skewed to be more like a diamond shape. Examples are dolomite and corundum.

¤ Orthorhombic crystals form rectangular prisms. Olivine and barite are two common examples.

¤ Monoclinic crystals look like tilted orthorhombic crystals. They tend to form long prisms. Many minerals crystallize in this system—gypsum, pyroxene, amphibole, malachite, orthoclase, and azurite, to name a few.

¤ Triclinic is the most irregular crystal form, where no two sides or angles are alike. Examples include plagioclase and axinite.

You can make models of each of the crystal systems. You'll need:

MATERIALS

¤ copy machine that can make enlargements	¤ paper
	¤ scissors
¤ heavy paper (cardstock quality) or lightweight cardboard (like cereal boxes)	¤ pencil
	¤ glue or clear tape

Make an enlarged copy of the crystal system templates on the following page.

One at a time, cut out the copied templates. (Do not cut this book.) Cut only around the outside lines.

Lay one cut-out on heavier paper and trace carefully around it. Remove the template and hand-copy its inside lines onto the traced shape on the heavier paper. These are guides to help you fold the shape into a 3-D crystal.

Fold each shape into a 3-D crystal. In each case, start at the box where four arms meet. Fold the four arms up to meet each other, making sharp creases along each of the lines. Glue or tape along the tabs to hold the crystal model in place. Finish folding along the remaining lines to close up the box.

With finished models in hand, look up examples of minerals that adopt that crystal form. Sometimes crystals form in shapes that look exactly like the models you made; sometimes they don't. Which ones look like your models? Which ones don't?

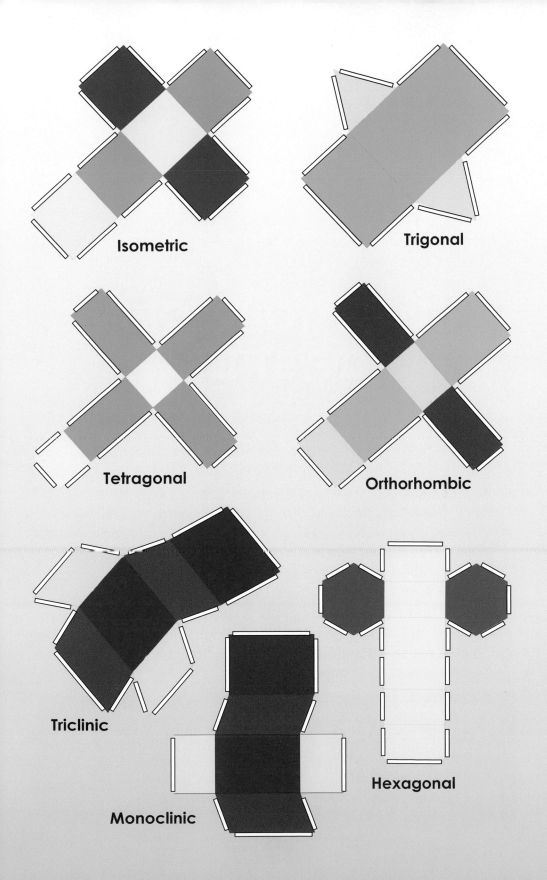

Isometric

Trigonal

Tetragonal

Orthorhombic

Triclinic

Hexagonal

Monoclinic

GROW YOUR OWN CRYSTALS

Though you may have to leave the formation of diamonds to nature, you can grow your own beautiful crystals from common nontoxic chemicals you can find in your kitchen or at the grocery store.

Easily grow crystals using any of the following simple, nontoxic compounds:

¤ Table salt (sodium chloride)

¤ Epsom salts (magnesium chloride)

¤ Alum (aluminum potassium sulfate)—Large, colorless alum crystals grow easily. Find alum in the spice aisle of your grocery store.

¤ Copper sulfate—Forms large, blocky, bright blue crystals. Find this chemical at pet stores and garden centers, where it is sold as an algae killer for aquariums and ponds.

MATERIALS	
¤ small amount (a few tablespoons or grams) of your compound of choice	¤ 2 clean jars
	¤ spoon
	¤ paper towel
	¤ fishing line
	¤ pencil
¤ ½ cup hot water	¤ tape

Pour the hot water into a jar. Stirring constantly, add the compound a little at a time until no more will dissolve.

Cover the jar with a paper towel and place it in a quiet place overnight.

The next day, remove the paper towel. Decant (pour slowly) the solution into a second jar, leaving tiny crystals behind on the bottom of the first jar. Tie a tiny loop at the end of a piece of fishing line, and use this to scoop up one of the "seed" crystals.

Lay a pencil over the mouth of the second jar. Drape the fishing line over the pencil so that the seed crystal hangs in the solution without touching the sides or bottom of the jar. Secure the fishing line to the pencil with tape so that the crystal stays put.

Cover the second jar with a paper towel and leave it in a quiet place. Check on your crystal each day.

Crystals grow best in a place that is free of dust and loud noise. Remember, too, that it takes time for molecules in the solution to bump into each other over and over. Only by chance will they arrange themselves in just the right way to begin the slow process of crystal formation.

GROW YOUR OWN SALT CRYSTAL GARDEN

This classic crystal-growing experiment uses a rough surface (charcoal) to help large crystals form quickly. Laundry bluing is a long, stringy molecule that keeps salt from forming boxy crystals, and encourages flower-like crystals to grow instead. Though this garden grows from useful household chemicals, it is not safe to eat! Keep it out of reach of pets and small children.

MATERIALS

- ¤ nonmetal container (such as glass baking dish or plastic storage box)
- ¤ charcoal briquets, broken into 1-inch pieces
- ¤ water (distilled, if possible)
- ¤ cup
- ¤ tablespoon
- ¤ uniodized table salt
- ¤ spoon
- ¤ ammonia
- ¤ laundry bluing (such as Mrs. Stewart's, found in grocery or hardware stores)
- ¤ food coloring

Dampen several charcoal pieces under running water. Shake off excess water and put the pieces in a nonmetal container.

Under **adult** supervision, combine 2 tablespoons salt with 4 tablespoons water in a cup, stirring to dissolve as much salt as possible. Add 2 tablespoons each of ammonia and laundry bluing, stirring until nothing else dissolves.

Pour the mixture, including any undissolved particles, over the damp charcoal. For a colorful garden, apply drops of food coloring to the briquets. Finally, sprinkle 2 tablespoons salt over the briquets and place the garden in a quiet spot.

Check on your crystal garden daily. You should see small crystals by the next day. You can then "feed" the garden and grow larger crystals, if you like, by adding a mixture of 2 tablespoons each salt, ammonia, and laundry bluing to the bottom of the container. Pores in the charcoal will carry the fresh solution up to the existing crystals.

When left protected and undisturbed, crystal gardens can be both beautiful and durable. This one was grown from a science kit over twenty years ago.

MAKE YOUR OWN GEODE

Occasionally a spherical hole can form inside rock, perhaps from bubbles trapped in magma, perhaps from a root ball that rotted away in sandstone. Over time, water carrying dissolved minerals finds its way into the hole. Mineral deposits line the sphere's walls, slowly filling in the hole with crystals in unique shapes and colors. The hardened ball of crystallized mineral, surrounded by a rocky shell, is called a geode.

Geodes are usually found as loose balls when the rock around them wears away. Like a present, only when the geode is opened (with a saw or rock hammer) can you know what lies inside. Understand how beautiful crystals form in this unique setting by making an "opened" geode in your own kitchen, using eggshells in place of rock shells.

MATERIALS

- ¤ eggs
- ¤ container (to store broken eggs)
- ¤ empty egg carton
- ¤ clean jar
- ¤ crystal-forming compound of choice (see Grow Your Own Crystals, page 38)
- ¤ hot water
- ¤ spoon
- ¤ food coloring (optional)

Carefully break the eggs around the center, keeping a straight line. Dump the eggs into a food storage container to cook with later.

Wash the eggshells and peel the slick membrane away from the interior. Place each half open-side up in the egg carton.

Make a supersaturated solution of your crystal-forming compound in a clean jar. Slowly add the compound to ½ cup hot water, stirring constantly, until no more will dissolve. Add food coloring if you like. Some compounds will incorporate the dye into their crystals, some will not. The eggshells will pick up the color.

Carefully pour the solution into the eggshells, until each is about three-quarters full.

Set the egg carton in a quiet place, checking on it every few days. When you are satisfied with your crystals, pour out the remaining solution.

Create your own crystals in a geode shape by pouring supersaturated crystal-forming solution carefully into the eggshell halves.

Books

DK Publishing. *Rocks and Minerals*. New York: Dorling Kindersley, 2008.

Farndon, John. *The Complete Illustrated Encyclopedia of Minerals, Rocks & Fossils of the World*. Bath, UK: Southwater, 2009.

Pellant, Chris. *Smithsonian Handbooks: Rocks and Minerals*. New York: Dorling Kindersley, 2002.

Stamper, Judith Bauer. *Rocky Road Trip: A Magic School Bus Chapter Book*. New York: Scholastic, 2003.

Zim, Herbert, and Paul Shaffer. *Rocks, Gems, and Minerals: A Golden Guide*. New York: St. Martins Press, 2001.

Works Consulted

Bonnet, Robert L., and G. Daniel Keen. *Earth Science: 49 Science Fair Projects*. Blue Ridge Summit, PA: Tab Books, Inc., 1990.

Booth, Jerry. *The Big Beast Book*. New York: Little, Brown and Co., 1988.

Deer, W.A., R.A. Howie, and J. Zussman. *An Introduction to the Rock-Forming Minerals*. Essex, UK: Addison Wesley Longman Limited, 1992.

Durham, Louise S. "The Elephant of All Elephants." *AAPG Explorer*, American Association of Petroleum Geologists, January 2005. http://www.aapg.org/explorer/2005/01jan/ghawar.cfm

Friedman, Herschel. "Mineral Resources: Finding Minerals." http://www.minerals.net/resource/finding.htm

Geological Society of America. http://geosociety.org.

Lawton, Rebecca, Diane Lawton, and Susan Panttaja. *Discover Nature in the Rocks*. Mechanicsburg, PA: Stackpole Books, 1997.

McMenamin, Mark A.S. *Science 101: Geology*. New York: HarperCollins, 2007.

Miller, William P., Rhett Jackson, and Todd Rasmussen. "Principles of Soil and Hydrology." University of Georgia. http://mulch.cropsoil.uga.edu/soilsandhydrology/index.htm

Pough, Frederick H. *Rocks and Minerals: The Peterson Field Guide Series*. Boston: Houghton Mifflin Company, 1988.

Ralph, Jolyon, and Ida Chau. "Mineralogy Database—Mineral Collecting, Localities, Mineral Photos, and Data." http://www.mindat.org

Schumann, Walter. *Minerals of the World*. Translated by Elisabeth E. Reinersmann. New York: Sterling Publishing Co., 1992.

The Science Company. "Crystal Experiments." http://www.sciencecompany.com/sci-exper/crystal_exp1.htm

Smith, Peter J., ed. *The Earth*. New York: Macmillan Publishing Company, 1986.

Topinka, Lyn. "Igneous Rocks." Cascades Volcano Observatory, United States Geological Survey. http://vulcan.wr.usgs.gov/LivingWith/VolcanicPast/Notes/igneous_rocks.html

University of Delaware Mineralogical Museum. http://www.udel.edu/museums/exhibitions/2009/mineralogical.html

Wetzel, David R. "Science Experiments with Rocks That Absorb Water." http://curriculalessons.suite101.com/article.cfm/how_to_find_out_if_rocks_absorb_water

On the Internet

Amethyst Galleries' Mineral Gallery
    http://www.galleries.com/
The Dynamic Earth at the National Museum of Natural History
    http://www.mnh.si.edu/earth/main_frames.html
Mineralogy Database
    http://www.mindat.org
Rock Hounds
    http://www.fi.edu/fellows/payton/rocks/index2.html
The Rock Key
    http://www.rockhounds.com/rockshop/rockkey/index.html
Rocks for Kids: Identifying Minerals
    http://www.rocksforkids.com/RFK/identification.html#Luster
San Diego Natural History Museum: Mineral Matters
    http://www.sdnhm.org/kids/minerals/index.html

Science Supply Companies

American Educational Products
    http://www.amep.com/
Carolina Biological Supply
    http://www.carolina.com/
Connecticut Valley Biological Supply Company
    http://www.ctvalleybio.com/
Edmund Scientific
    http://scientificsonline.com/
Nasco
    http://www.enasco.com/
WARD'S Natural Science
    http://wardsci.com/

PHOTO CREDITS: Cover, pp. 5, 9, 15, 37, 39, 43—CreativeCommons; p. I—JupiterImages; pp. 13, 19, 22, 24, 27, 28, 34, 4I—Claire O'Neal; p. 26—Sharon Beck. Every effort has been made to locate all copyright holders of material used in this book. If any errors or omissions have occurred, corrections will be made in future editions of the book.

cementation (see-men-TAY-shun)—Forming chemical bonds that "glue" grains together to make rock.

composition (kom-poh-ZIH-shun)—The makeup or formula of something.

crystal habit (KRIH-stul HAB-it)—The visible pattern a crystal follows as it forms.

crystal system—The pattern the molecules follow as a crystal forms.

dodecahedron (doh-dek-uh-HEE-drun)—A three-dimensional shape with twelve identical sides.

element (EL-uh-munt)—The simplest chemical substance, consisting of only one kind of atom.

erosion (ee-ROH-zhun)—The moving of rock or other ground materials by water, wind, or ice.

geode (JEE-ohd)—A rock with an inner space in which crystals have formed.

heft—Perceived weight.

igneous (IG-nee-us) **rock**—Rock that has formed from cooled lava or magma.

lithification (lih-thih-fih-KAY-shun)—The pressing or hardening of a substance into rock.

luster (LUS-tur)—The degree to which light reflects from a mineral, causing it to shine.

metamorphic (meh-tuh-MOR-fik) **rock**—Rocks that have changed through intense heat and pressure over time.

plutonic (ploo-TAH-nik) **rock**—Igneous rock formed from hardened magma.

porosity (por-AH-sih-tee)—The amount and size of the pores, or holes, in an object.

principle of superposition (PRIN-sih-pul of soo-per-poh-ZIH-sun)—The rule of thumb followed by geologists that in layers of sedimentary rocks, the oldest layers were deposited first.

rock cycle—The ability of one rock type (sedimentary, igneous, metamorphic) to change into another rock type when subjected to earth's forces.

sediment (SEH-duh-munt)—Particles or grains of rock deposited by erosion.

sedimentary (SEH-duh-ment-ur-ee) **rock**—Rock that forms from sediments.

strata (STRAT-uh)—Layers of rock.

supersaturated (SOO-pur-SAA-chur-ay-ted)—The condition of a solution in which no more particles can dissolve.

volcanic (vol-KAH-nik) **rock**—Igneous rock formed from hardened lava.

weathering (WEH-thur-ing)—The chemical or physical breakdown of rock by water, wind, or ice.

acid test 31–32
andesite 6
apatite 26
barite 36
basalt 4, 6
breccia 13
calcite 16, 26, 30, 31–32, 35
cementation 4, 6, 12, 31
clay 10, 13, 14
collecting, rock 20–22
conglomerate 13
crystal 4–6
    garden 40–41
    habit 24
    shape 24, 38–39
    system 35–36, 37
diamond 25, 26, 35, 38
diolite 5
dolomite 31, 32, 36
erosion 13, 15–16
feldspar 26
fluorite 26, 27
fossils 10, 12
gabbro 5
galena 28
gemstones 4, 24, 26, 35
geodes 42–43
gneiss 6
gold 24
granite 4, 5, 6
graphite 28, 29
gravel 14, 17
gypsum 26, 36
halite (salt) 33–34, 35
hardness 25, 26, 27–28
heft 29, 30
hematite 24, 28
hornblende 28
ice 15, 16, 17, 35
igneous rocks 4–6, 7, 8, 16, 17
lava 6, 17
limestone 4, 6, 10, 11, 15, 18, 31
lithification 6, 8, 13, 17
luster 24
magma 4–6, 7, 42

magnetite 24, 28, 30
marble 4, 32
metamorphic rocks 6, 7, 9, 16, 17
mica, muscovite 24
minerals, everyday uses of 4, 32
Mohs, Friedrich 25
Mohs scale (see hardness)
obsidian 6
olivine 36
pebbles 11, 13
plutonic rocks 4–5
porosity 17–19
principle of superposition 10, 11
pumice 6, 17
pyrite 24, 28, 35
quartz 26, 28, 30, 35
rhyolite 6
rock cycle 7–9
rock kit 6
ruby 26
sand 6, 10, 11, 14
sandstone 6, 11, 12, 42
schist 6
scoria 6
sediment 6, 7, 8, 13
sedimentary rocks 6, 7, 8, 10–12, 17, 31
shale 6, 13
silt 10, 14
siltstone 10, 12
silver 24
slate 6
specific gravity 29–30
steel 4
strata 10–12
streak 27–28
sulfur 28
talc 25, 26, 27
topaz 26
volcanoes 5–6
weathering (see erosion)
zircon 35

As a child, Claire O'Neal enjoyed collecting rocks and minerals with her brother. Her favorite specimen was a big purple fluorite octahedron she collected from a mine in southern Illinois. Though she grew up to study English, biology, and chemistry at college, she secretly loved rocks so much that she married a geologist. Today, she is a versatile author, having published a dozen books with Mitchell Lane in addition to professional scientific papers. She lives in Delaware with her husband, two young sons, and a fat black cat.